EARTHQUAKE WEATHER

KNIGHT-CAPRON LIBRARY

Thornton Writer-in-Residence

Spring 1997

EARTHQUAKE WEATHER

August Kleinzahler

MOYER BELL LIMITED
MOUNT KISCO, NEW YORK

Published in the United States and Canada
by Moyer Bell Limited
Copyright © 1989 August Kleinzahler

All rights reserved. No part of this publication may be reproduced, stored in a retrieval system or transmitted, in any form or by any means, electronic, mechanical, photocopying, recording or otherwise, without the prior written permission of Moyer Bell Limited, Colonial Hill, Mt. Kisco, New York 10549.

The author wishes to acknowledge the generous assistance of the New Jersey State Council on the Arts.

Some of these poems first appeared in the following magazines: *B-City, The Berkeley Poetry Review, Brief, 89¢, Epoch, Figs, Giants Play Well in the Drizzle, Harper's, Meanjin, New American Writing, The New Yorker, Ninth Decade, Numbers, Occident, OINK!, Origin, Ploughshares, Poetry Flash, Scripsi, Sulfur, The Threepenny Review,* and *ZYZZYVA*

"The Gardenia" was first issued as a Dreadnaught Press broadside for the Canadian National Book Festival, Toronto, 1982

"Winter Branches I" was originally issued as "Maple, Oak in Winter Sky," a broadside from *imprimerie dromadaire,* Toronto, 1986

"Soda Water with a Boyhood Friend" appeared in *Best American Poetry: 1988,* edited by John Ashbery, Scribners, 1988

Some of these poems, in variant forms, appeared previously in:
A Calendar of Airs, The Coach House Press, Toronto, 1978
Dainties&Viands, Galloping Dog Press, Newcastle Upon Tyne, 1985
Blue at 4 P.M., Northern Lights, London, 1986
Six More, twobitter, LETTERS, Toronto, 1987
The Last Big Snow, Northern Lights, London, 1988
On Johnny's Time, Pig Press, Durham, 1988

Cover photo courtesy of the California Historical Society, San Francisco. FN-14905

Library of Congress Cataloging-in-Publication Data
Kleinzahler, August.
    Earthquake weather / by August Kleinzahler.
    p.   cm.
    ISBN 0-918825-97-0   ISBN 0-918825-98-9 (pbk.)
    I. Title.
PR9199.3.K482E37   1989
811'.54—dc19   88-34431
                                                                                      CIP

Printed in the United States of America

CONTENTS

I

Love Poem · 13
Earthquake Weather · 14
On Johnny's Time · 16
Sunday in November · 17
English as a Second Language · 18
Nurses and Comedians · 19
Work · 20
Lock Shop · 21
Bay Lullaby · 22
Disappointment · 23
His Neighbor, Her Music · 24
Old Movies · 25
April Before Gehenna · 26
The Lunatic of Lindley Meadow · 27
Afternoons · 28
Outing · 30
A Little July Something · 31
Tuesday Morning · 32
Sunday in September · 33
What it Takes · 34
Late Indian Summer · 35
Ebenezer Californicus · 36
Friends Through at New Year's · 37

II

Blue at 4 P.M. · 41
The Last Big Snow · 42
Winter Branches I · 43
Soda Water with a Boyhood Friend · 44
Water&Ice · 45

Winter Branches II · 46
Playing Hooky at the Natural History Museum · 47
1978: Montreal · 48
Where Galluccio Lived · 50
Like Cities, Like Storms · 51
On the Way Home to Jersey One Night · 52
Family Album · 53

III

The Tree · 57
The Fourth of July · 58
Pinned · 60
The Gardenia · 61
Four Worthies
    I   Tranter in America · 62
    II   A Birthday Bash for Thomas Nashe · 64
    III A Baroque Scot's Excess · 65
    IV Hootie Bill Do Polonius · 66
Before Winter · 68
Before Winter, Part II · 69
Before Winter, Part III · 70
Lint · 72
Hack · 73
Song · 74
Art&Life · 75
Since You Didn't Phone · 79
Sunset in Chinatown · 78

In memory of Basil Bunting
and Thelonious Monk

It tastes good, garlic and salt in it,
with the half-sweet white wine of Orvieto
on scanty grass under great trees
where the ramparts cuddle Lucca.

It sounds right, spoken on the ridge
between marine olives and hillside
blue figs, under the breeze fresh
with pollen of Apennine sage.

It feels soft, weed thick in the cave
and the smooth wet riddance of Antonietta's
bathing suit, mouth ajar for
submarine Amalfitan kisses.

It looks well on the page, but never
well enough. Something is lost
when wind, sun, sea upbraid
justly an unconvinced deserter.

> from *Briggflatts*

I heard about this Felonius guy—he's some
kinda nut. He'll come in a club and stare at
a wall. I mean, he's not like Erroll Garner or
Oscar Peterson—he can't sit down and play
you a regular show. Besides which, I hear he
never gets out of New Jersey somewheres.

> attributed to the owner of the
> Black Hawk Jazz Club in San Francisco, 1958

EARTHQUAKE WEATHER

I

Love Poem

As long as the cat comes home
and the skinheads keep
to their concrete shell, over the fence
screaming *break your face,* smashing empties

what need is there to worry or come undone
so the wolf slips in,
cutting through us like cheese, soft cheese
an emulsion of blood and cheese

except for the radio tower close by
blighting *Ruby, My Dear*
till you shift in your chair and it's right,
both speakers, all there . . .

Poor Monk, dying at the Baroness's
on the hill above Weehawken
night after night
cars sluicing into the tunnel below

into the city, fanning lights
across the broad river,
the West Side throbbing
across black water

out of notes, dying.

Earthquake Weather

She's talking to herself
or somebody
spasm talk
heaving
broken apart
as it escapes her weather

She can slip in there
when the air's right
and lay her stripe down
red
along your nerve-snake's sheathing

Mrs B
she forgot her medication
now she's *on*
flinching
at the rejoinder
or blow

matted hair
and chewed red nose
that's her
hard done by
. . . husband
mother . . .
cruel fat daughter
money
always money

pleading her case down Clayton
solo
in the fog
past the old Lab'
puzzling her scent through
Mrs B

faces staring
as the bus makes its turn
she'll lay her stripe down
when the air gets still
she'll slip right in
and make you breathe
wrong

On Johnny's Time

When Johnny goes out
he's careful what gets into his Time.
He likes Time plain,
the better to taste it run out of him
like water out holes
in the Old Town's corroded pipe.

— *What sort of business you in?*
the good burgher always asks John.
— *Monkeybusiness,* is what John likes to tell him,
and won't crack a smile, ever.
That's John.
But when Johnny goes out

on Johnny's own Time
he's out there doing the only one thing:
he's burning off all the still-born Johnnys
that hatched in his head in the night.
And that John, he won't ever come home,
not until he's right.

Sunday in November

And who were they all in your sleep last night
    chattering so
you'd think that when you woke
the living room would be full of friends and ghosts?

But you see, nobody's here, no one but you
    and the room's nearly bare
except for Paddy's playstring all covered in dust
and a bottle of tinted air.

Pop and Lola, the sullen, little clerk from the store,
    and eight or ten more. Now
which were the dream ones and who did you meet that was
    real?
You were, for the most part, you.

Such a big room: how nice to be alone in it
    with the one lit bulb and dying plant,
the day so large and gray outside,
dogs running through it in circles, buses, shouts.

And later on where will you take her?
    Up to the rock. And what will you see there?
Roofs and the bay. Have you a song to sing her?
The wind will do and she'll think it's me.

But who were they all in your sleep last night
    first one then the next
with their menace, wild semaphore, and lusts?
I hardly know where you find the strength

come morning.

English as a Second Language

Ship
I wrote   on the empty blackboard

and the turbine salesman from Mitsubishi
wrote it down too

Ship
Noun and verb, I told him

Ship
We **shipped** a turbine to San Francisco

Sip, said the man with the 3–diamond stickpin

Shhip, I said back with bracing correctness

But even as I spoke an impulse skipped

    I heard the word new

        sound   cut in space

      not this thing   or that

            purely

Ship

Ship, I said vaguely

Ummm   **shhip**, said my student with gravity

(Ummm   ve-ry im-por-tant word), he concluded
under his breath

Nurses and Comedians

Student nurses all in a row
waiting for apples and cakes:
their phonemes mix with air
and turn into a swarm of pink flies;

the flies turn into words: *Hi Hi Hi,*
Mao had the char peis all put to sleep —
capitalist playthings, *he said;*
but their skin is so velvety I love them . . .

Young comics are mean,
frantic to make electrons scream
in your palm, behind your knee,
plundering the house for laughter

only to be caught in the bounteous waters
streaming from Child-Nurse: so
sudden and unlike,
so much more than anything — Mao,

disporting in the Yangtze —

anything the feverish young comics have known.

Work

The sweep-up man stinks of cologne
while the boss is on
about a piece in Sacramento
could really *snatch* it
back, oh, in '58.

Sun lower after work
and a pretty face
starting to melt suggests you twig
the big canvas,

but it's only a post card
from an age gone by
of the plump grande dame
her wistful gaze

nearly attractive
but the focus not quite soft enough.

Lock Shop

Frank punched steel stamps into key bows
then duped them on the grinder
for thirty-odd years,
just to keep off from dead-bolt or cylinder work.
He never did learn how to locksmith —

thirty-odd years and the old nail pounder
still couldn't figure it out:
just the hammer, drill, and a big smile
for whatever lady it was up front.
Besides, he liked how hard metal bit into soft.

The last day Frank wore powder-blue dacron slacks
and a necktie with little birds knit on.
He had coffee like always with the machinists at break,
kissed both secretaries, kissed DeLois
     at the Trouble Desk,
and left.

    Now John says he's had it;
took a job in the desert, down around Blythe:
a new correction facility
not a hundred miles from that land he bought
right along the Colorado.
He'll still be State so won't hurt on his pension.

John used to locksmith over at Vacaville,
the biggest prison on earth.
Told me how one time there he ran onto Charlie Manson.
— *Was he crazy?* I asked.

— *Crazy?* John says and gives me this look.

                Crazy?

— *Hell yes, he was crazy.*

Bay Lullaby

Tuesdays are bad for sausage and flowers
rain
sweeping in off the sea, foghorns
lowing like outsize beasts
shackled to cliffs at the mouth of the Bay

You hear them from under the movie marquee
before going in to dry
off in plush, alone
behind two old ladies, that song of a wanton from long ago
Temptation, filling the empty room

Across the city's northwest quadrant
two, maybe three miles in
drifting through holes in the traffic and rain
you hear them warning ships off the rocks
moaning like fettered gods

Lilies begun to curl
and meat gone sad at the delicatessen
trays of wurst
fat seeping into the skins
before Thursday delivery and the big weekend

As morning's first trolley clears the track
the cat's petite snores
her upper lip's cleft beaded with sweat
you still hear them out there in the dark
mingling their calls in the rain

Disappointment

A faint smell of urine
embroidering that bouquet of mold the big cushions
give off days the fog won't lift,

and a shelf of bone
growing out over the eyelids like evening's shadow
across a field of corn —

The whole parade
leaking out from your shoulders, bequeathing
to the groin a pang of distance;

then that metallic taste in the mouth
and a voice you had let yourself believe
was dead

close now by your ear, intimate and sweet:

          Well, well, well,
look what we have here.

His Neighbor, Her Music

The hermaphrodite with ginger hair
and scarlet tights
            straining,
scalding its larynx
for that note old subways make, metal
on metal

    . . . goosing the volume
till our own air shakes —

her *last chance* implement:
screams
                piercing
that hide of face Kool after Kool's
stuck into, pulled
out

folds of sallow mist her liver
raised
    clouding the eyes
after how many parties Tuesday
night

Old Movies

Fueled with violins, the luscious soundtrack
pulls the old movie down the line
with its cargo of lovers   limo   and guns
till our hearts break
and the exit doors open on goodness and hope.

Good-bye, my love, good-bye.
Light pricks us
and we bleed from a thousand tiny holes
opalescent air draining out of us
night rushing in.

April Before Gehenna

My neighbor went down to Haight for to preach
and I followed him down for my pint.
Buses parted swarms of shoppers.
Dusk swirled in on a twenty knot wind
settling on parapet moldings
ornate and quirky as a child's crayon street.

— *The end is nigh,* my neighbor told them,
the haggard young men
shuffling in doorways, working to keep warm.
And maybe he's right,
just as when he told me tiny ponds of Miller High Life
is a fool way to kill snails.

So these final days I spend alone, walking
in the hills below Twin Peaks
and on the hidden stairways connecting streets
crowded by poppies, valeriana
profuse as weeds among Lily-of-the-Nile
and bottlebrush stamens flaring.

Faith wanting, I only seek to empty my mind:
sun fueling my pineal gland
against long winter nights; tranced
by which bloom's which, or one Schnauzer sniffing
another, and whether the fog bank sitting off shore
rolls in at 5.

The Lunatic of Lindley Meadow

At nightfall, when the inquisitive elves in elf-pants
wander over the ridge with chummy screed,
the snaps of the beak your hand becomes cease,

and evening's last fungo dwindles
high over the spruce, for an instant getting lost
in one band of sky turning dark under another,

falling back into view falling
out of the sky, *pop*, a dead wren in his mitt. *Let's
get home*, the big boy says, *Mom'll holler.*

The car horns along Fulton subside with the dark,
the big felt-lined dark: bright little logos and cars
set in black felt while still pulsing light,

a lid on top. And see, here he comes now,
Conga Lad, pleasing the elves who come close but not too,
making the birds go way. Time to start home,

so clean it up nice and blow germs off your pouch —
the nice warm room, the smell in the wool.

Afternoons

Young Mitch jumps off the 7 Haight in black Toreadors.
Hard to say which film did it;
most likely something peppy and fun from the early 60's:
a youthful Janet Leigh, like that.

* * *

> "I HEARD A CHILD'S CRY IN THE RUBBLE"
> Millbrae Mom Collapses In Grief

Dear Mr. Hearst,

    There is no war here.
I would like to come home.

    Yours sincerely,

    Frederic Remington

* * *

The first few weeks the fog scared her.
All that spring she'd had Wednesdays off
and never missed a matinée:
                      the only clean cool place
in town to hide, the Rialto.

Last show she caught before heading West, a real chiller
and no cartoons,
    The Fog.

— *Are you frightened?*
he asked, the two of them under the ridge, wind
picking up in advance of it,
still too shy to touch:
    or just cold?

Outing

If I pull out the jack
and be still
    till my friend peeks out

from under my hat and runs off
to prowl, keep
low or go wild in the lot

overgrown with foxtail, then stays
away two nights
and a day don't let's not . . .

Just dim the lights, draw
the blind
and give us a bagatelle in F

yes, F would be nice
till you hear a scrrr-atch at the back
door and lookie

see

A Little July Something

Whose muse?   The pigeon
flew
     clear of the claw, just
and left us some few feathers

early,
before the alarm goes off and
then the cars.

          In at the eye
and out the back of my head —
(note: putty)

          fine grains,
the whole goddam tableau
fine grains

exposed by sunlight through a
hole (*putty*)
          and sifting

into dust devils.   DUST DEVILS —

not the hawthorn tree's bright berry
nor the long legs

          Excuse me, Miss
those purple flowers
on the tree there, you
wouldn't . . .
          attached to . . . umm humm
in shades
     reading Colette
stretched out at such length, so . . . so . . .
DUST DEVILS, it's you

Tuesday Morning

I like you!

                     (signed) *God*

it reads in white
script against a field of blue, dark
blue
    painted on the side
of an old brick residence hotel

as the 6 Parnassus
turns
    onto Market a sexual revery
    drifts
by like a whiff of drugstore perfume

pulling warm blood down after it
even as we
        check the boxscores
from last night

eyes
streaming from fatigue or grief too
remote
    to find among discount palaces
and workers steaming cobbles

we step down
        tearful, erect

into the cool gray early morning

Sunday in September

O I dunno Ma walk around town I guess
check out the arugula at Tony Pro's

then head along to the sea and back
or what the sky has going

late one Sunday afternoon toward fall
high over the Panhandle and college spires

gray as ever but just now another gray
ask Turner — Turner *Who&How Much*?

air cooler and the breeze very fresh
you peek into the half-light

of a corner bar, color TV flickering
heads bent over drink or tilted up

in ritual tropisms of talk or the game —
a diorama the new museum paid too much for

What It Takes

He stared for hours
at the cat
taking his ease under the calla leaf
or fog
pour in late afternoon
whelming the tower on the hill

how bird   truck   or shout
wind&light
scored day the way the music
roll in a nickelodeon's scored
and what it played in the mind

or the young Bill Evans
before Scott LaFaro died
playing
  My Foolish Heart
again and again
fennel, lobelia   shadow&flies

however many times it takes

Late Indian Summer

The rains hold off another week,
and the midday heat,
long after the winegrapes are in, has the cat
sprawled flat under the jade plant.

Nights already belong to winter.
You know by that tuning fork in its jacket
of bone
broadcasting to the body's far ports.

Days like this so late in the year
inflame desire, perturb
the ground of dreams, and roust us from sleep
exhausted and stunned.

Ebenezer Californicus

Don't make me go out eat goose
be nice get a headache
all right?
because the sun's so strong
so warm delish the back of my neck
making mutinous the wee city-states
that dot it —
goosebumps of intrigue, of the possible

Terrible people
up&down the street terrible people
smiling
    the smiles of greed
    the mooncalf's grin
    the Bob Hope Holiday Leer of Delight
the smile of the broken,
hurt
    pullulating:
    not six weeks out of the can
    like drunk at 8 A.M.

    that smile

— Maddy crifsmuss, brudder
Stare shhange?
        O Christ
O
   Merry WhackWhack, Mrs QuackQuack

    Write soon

        Love

        Baby Teapot

Friends Through at New Year's

The old year's calendars flutter down
in the mist,
        countless sheets
of dated memoranda escorting them like pilot fish
to the street below

as friends pass through, alone and with kids:
the one down from Juneau
headed south to Belize for the diving;
and the clan from Vancouver, two little girls now
and a grubstake to buy a boat with, sail
the islands off of Crete, Turkey maybe, just way
the hell away from housepainting and rain.

We watch cartoons as front after front
sweeps through,
        worse than Vancouver.   — *This is worse
than Vancouver*, she says,
but they all go to the carousel in the park anyhow
and catch cold
because the big one remembers from last time.

The other friend is drinking, talking
about the woman back up in Sitka, how the last letter
was strange;
        and her youngest boy, Tom,
the way the two of them got along.

When old friends speak of the past
after the years apart, lives so different,
                              how well

they seem to know us, still,
after such a long time, better than our families,
our lovers.
          So much of ourselves that we had forgotten
alive in them still

whose children fall asleep in our arms.

II

Blue at 4 P.M.

The burnish of late afternoons
as winter ends —
this sadness coming on in waves is not round
and sweet
as the doleful cello

but jagged, intent
finding out places to get through the way wind
tries seams
and cracks of the old house, making
the furnace kick on

or the way his trumpet
sharks
through cloud and paradise shoal, nosing
out the dark fillet
to tear apart and drink his own

The Last Big Snow

                She snowed
a night, a day
and another night, laying down deafness
as she went
and deafness again on top of
what she had let down
as she wound continually out of herself.

               And when she was done
she pulled
a wind onto the town, routing
snow into spindrift
off the mortar between bricks,
then blowing it back down.
                         Cats
threw cats
      off each shed's sweetest angle.

The week that freighters slept in the ice
a day from port,
and the dove at our window
coo'd till first light,
my love gave herself over to making a broth.
With the fluid and pith of pale legumes
she came on a savor
               that visited our rooms
like a certain thought.

Those nights near the turning
when beacons on snowplows flashed until dawn,
and caravans of trucks
brought snow to the river as snow fell
on the river,
my love gave herself over to the making of broth
while I, in turn,
stirred until thick my greasy soup.

Winter Branches

(I)

A section of cortex
stained dark and frozen on a field
of gray
       axons, dendrites
probe and reticulate
               layered

as the frigid river's gray no
one sings of
       mighty

almighty oak
&maple
sleeved with snow voices nipple

into which . . .
           I don't want to
trace it out
like junior high school I

don't get paid
       to   *huhrr*   *huhrr*
hhhh-ump out all

eighteen fleurs punched into
this mine breastbone
              coming

    up&over
what fence came last, we're off
our own trim caravel

sleek
      and cut down
to a hunting
        thang

Soda Water with a Boyhood Friend

He is in the canals behind your forehead
paddling,
        or in the high vaulted rooms
your speech
rays around itself, checking
the physics
of a dropped dime
resonating against what he has down
in the log of his remembering . . .

over a cigar and club soda. Ah,
the forests,
the good jungle, deluged with scene mutating
scene breeding scene,
fuckingchoking to death —
a regular Mardi Gras on LSD
wired into your EEG
and beamed off satellite
to multitudes of kindled selves.

Water&Ice

A hawk wind locks up runnels in ice
till the sun burns through
            finding them out.
Then you hear underfoot as the wind comes back
a tightening,
            leaving behind patterns change makes
on the surface
you can read as a sailor reads the face
of the sea.

Light, the world underfoot,
changing . . .
            A keening wind moves through
raising chords
as if our sternum and ribs were strung
like a harp.

Winter Branches
(II)

. . .
or a net of capillaries, veins, the full moon
beats through
        the sky late winter
between sunset and night

more clarifying to the spirit
than the ancient Chinese glazes, tea dust,
        plum shade,
the celadons from Hangchow

that take hold of the mind,
fastening it;
        and when a bird shoots through
between shadow and snow, branch and roof,

the heart tracks it
washed in a pleasure so distilled,
        so exquisite and sharp,
as to seem a kind of ecstasy

                              (for Ralph Mills, Jr.)

Playing Hooky
at the Natural History Museum

Upstairs from the pretzel booth, turnstiles
      and lacerating squeaks
of the E–train, double–A local and F
we go again to the South Island Alps.

The kakapo is there by the alpine lake,
      the pied fantail too.
Untroubled in the shadows thrown by moa feet,
behemoth feet, with knobs,

how bright and calm they look.
      The moa's tiny head,
at such remove from earth, cocks alert to a tone
or good scent off the set.

In a place where the feet belong only to birds
      who is there to step on
the toe or slice the throat which, Seuss-like,
sprouts from that flightless hulk?

Just out of view, on the opposite shore, Her Majesty
      's vassals in sleek long boats
clubs at the ready push off,
intent to stuff imagination . . .

1978: Montreal

                    She took the radio.

Wind
breaches the coping, whining
and soughing
in the bathroom shaft.

Down the same shaft old TV westerns
in French:
           — *Allons,*
           Monsieur Hopalong.

From below
hollering and moans: Mrs. Mooney's
gentleman is unwell —
dark, grievous sounds,
as if a proctoscope approached
the rotten truth.

The stairs happen all night:
women's steps,
                busy and light,
syncopated;
loping men,
a pause on the landing and off.

Another three months and then the heat,
the haze,
when sweat pools in the small
of the back —

        and a radio,
with dials,
dials that glow . . .
              Nights
on the balcony —

and across the roofs of the east end
up the corridor of Vermont
twi-night doubleheaders
from Fenway Park,
              beer jingles
fading in
      and out.

Where Galluccio Lived

Get all of it, boys,
every brick,
so the next big storm blows out
any ghost left with the dust.

In that closet of air the river
wind gnaws at
was where the crucifix hung;
and over there

by the radio and nails,
that's where Galluccio kept
with his busted leg
in an old, soft chair

watching TV and the cars
go past.

       Whole floors,
broken up and carted off . . .

Memory stinks,
like good marinara sauce.
You never get that garlic smell
out of the walls.

Like Cities, Like Storms

Like cities, like storms

these alto and tenormen
blow back cool legato or a rope of cries
against a world pouring down
so hard and fast

the bass and drums are about to fly
off the beat
and lose the soloist orbiting
round it

but don't, somehow
thirty, forty years ago at the Royal
Roost, Five Spot or studio
in Hackensack.

With the owner counting heads
and the kid
down from Yale working his way up
his girlfriend's thigh

the rhythm men keep holding on

a foot off the ground,
but holding.

On the Way Home to Jersey One Night

The same sad stories whip around
and around
streaking the air between dark buildings,
breaking apart in the updraft.

A million tough chances
and Dina's bad back —
galaxies, nebulae of tired old destinies
flying apart in the wind:

the wind off the Hudson,
wrapping itself round the Hotel New Yorker,
riding the aluminum twigs
of a cyclone fence —

something about the wind,
how it roots around in the passageways and lots,
a kind of animal;
and in the night itself,

so dark,
as if everything had been washed out of it —
absence, a terrible absence,
like space.

And the two guys from Chicago,
Algren and Farrell —
I'm always imagining them out there
in the shadows and doorways,

at every window and busted skylight,
keeping the ledger,

taking the last soiled scraps of it in.

Family Album

Loneliness — huge, suddenly menacing
and no one is left here who knows me anymore:
the Little League coach,
his TV repair truck and stinking cigars
and Saul the Butcherman
and the broken arm that fell out of the apple tree
dead
dead or gone south to die warm

The little boy with mittens and dog
posing on the stoop —
he isn't me;
and the young couple in polo shirts, ready to pop
with their firstborn
four pages on in shortshorts and beatnik top
showing her figure off at 16 . . .
1955 is in an attic bookcase
spine cracked and pages falling out

Willow and plum tree
green pods from maple whirling down to the sidewalk . . .
Only the guy at the hot dog stand since when
maybe remembers me,
or at least looks twice

But the smushfaced bus from New York, dropping
them off at night along
these avenues of brick somber as the dead child
and crimes of old mayors
lets off no one I know, or want to

Warm grass and dragonflies —
O, my heart

III

The Tree

Pinch a branch to see if it's quick
or else the thing 'll just stand
for who knows how long
sun, wind, frost, chafing it, dogs
pissing at the base
birds nesting up high where leaves had been

while the years blur
and the town next door 's evacuated
so the kids don't turn stupid
from the water that solvents leached into
or testicle cancer
diagnosed in the Mayor on down

Cape Canaveral is renamed Eric Dolphy
your friends all swell, turn
ugly then drop
after their cute little girls grow up to fuck brutes
marry them and breed

but that shield of bark
photons roam the grain of
and pathogens try to corkscrew into
only to fall apart and dry. . .

because it would not bloom
because it would not die

the axman came

The Fourth of July

Mountain blue on the powerline,
preening
as the big C-119 heads out low over aspen
and yellow pine, dragging
slurry to Challis, up by Yankee Fork.

Idaho is burning.
Hot dogs on sale at The Merc:
pleasure craft
tearing apart the morning lake
send osprey wheeling toward deeper woods.

Aspen, osprey —
haze over half the state;
on TV
the Atlanta infield green as old Technicolor
while cool still in the front room.

Under how many roofs, domes
of sky —
the basement outside Juneau,
mud and stinking tap water;
the swish flat in Brooklyn Heights . . .

Two boys on the ferry north
out of Seattle spring '73, hardened, primed
to stoke their souls;
the books the fear the girls
reduced to a map of where they had to go.

The smoke jumper passes a joint
between boats
to his pilot, your old lady's ex,
fireworks exploding into bloom overhead,
colored flares dying before they hit the lake.

You say how it's like *acid*, you
don't know
what it is supposed to happen next anymore.
I tell you I'm fried,
how this last year kicked hell out of me.

Past novelty and charm,
the best moves left for strangers,
moves to buy time,
we drink, sneaking looks at one another,
friend at friend,

each more and more coming to resemble his father.

Pinned

The ways water finds to undo
   the bonds of solid things:

you move across my flank,
   the ground turns strange;
your sylph-gang churns a breeze
   and my beanie's propeller
ticks the air morosely;
   two steps and I'm out of breath;
morsels of scrod and aspic
   drop unchewed to my plate.

Wrestlers work this way:
   they uproot you from earth
and take you back down,
   tied insolubly to their wills.

The Gardenia

Corinna in May pushed a rusty nail
deep in the soil of her sick gardenia.

All through the rain months leaf tips curled.
What buds appeared were sickly pale.
As a consumptive heroine in winter light
so fared and failed Corinna's plant.

In June, beside the burbling toilet,
a dark shellac arose in the leaves.
A bud grew fat and began to peel.
The pedicel swelled.

At last came the bloom.

Corinna of the milky thighs
unfastened her wrapper and drew a bath
so that she might wash, dream
then wash herself again

that warm spring night in the fragrant room.

Four Worthies

I Tranter in America

In the jelly, jam, and haircare aisle of the Waikiki Safeway
as if in a capsule whose walls bear decals, a shattered fresco
(*Fatty Arbuckle sipping a Coke at the St. Francis Hotel*, etc.)
the Man from Moruya, a world then a world away again from
   the chrysanthemums
at the farm's eastern gate, is turned inward by The Percy Faith
   Strings'
arrangement of an especial old favorite, "Just Like Tom
   Thumb's Blues" —
iridescent oil pouring from the overhead speakers, lubricating
the sentiment *we're all, each of us, one, softening*
and put somehow more at ease by the very available and high-
   gloss kitsch
the Big Enchilada loves you to hate

or out on the highway, four miles from town, on a stool in the
   Snack Bar
of Empire Lanes, sneering as the pins go down, all at once and
   on cue,
with an almighty crack radiating out from Pawtucket to
   Geyserville;
and you knock back a codeine between gulps of fries as the TV
   overhead
shows a rerun of *Kojak* you saw a decade ago in a Canberra
   motel.
You are drifting, drifting ever further from Frank O'Hara's
   Lower East Side flat

where you sit daydreaming: it is 1959 and you are staring out
    the window
at a finny Bel Air scarred rather nicely by kids or sleet, parked
on a billboard across the street kittycorner to a Nedick's,
the orange drink tumbling and roiling in its smudged plastic
    tank
a slow, piss-scented elevator ride up from the cavern
Grendel in warpaint flashes and roars through
and from which the frail sonneteer and critic of ballet
will emerge in twenty-three minutes to knock ever so
    delicately
just in time for a spot of Jim Beam to keep off the chill, the
    first
of September, as Frank puts the final touch to *Poem*
the one beginning "Khruschev is coming on the right day!"
then kicks open the door to his study and, breathless as the
    young Rita Hayworth
after a terrible fright, cries out   — *We're on with de Kooning*
for a tequila sunrise at eight, then ... How is everyone? All
    right?

II A Birthday Bash for Thomas Nashe

Rapscallion Nashe jumped
o'er jumped
the ornate gait
and hop pitty hopped through the field

Say
    such wiggy proportions blow
    the Scheme of Most Harmonious He
or
    a rude rough masque 't would make
    for the court of the Greasy Gobb'd King

Hell what's hot too hot to touch
is hotter still to hold
But *you* grab a piece of street
or a strumpet's hank

then insert a Senecan
bromide (maybe on déshabillé and scruples). Can
a spot noplace be found
not in the mare's nosebag or worked

into the filigree
of a smooth Florentine's shiv? Nashe can
in that sublime and rat-strewn wreck
of lutes and savaged bears

O, many are the pantaloons since unravelled
and dead 4 centuries
                    Harvey the Vilifier
... Who?
        While still boss, startling

and rash

            Your Honour's in all humble service:
                    Tho: Nashe

III A Baroque Scot's Excess

Sir Thomas Urquhart, Knight
found a puddle
outside the Cat&Mustard pot
sat
and waged pitiful tyranny
against the phlegm,
vibrato and tears that bespoke drink
on a heavy heart

shook him
with a meaty hiccup
up a foot
then dropped him
smartly
on the coccyx.
His bottom lip tumefied
into a pout:
        This knight is poorly,

Tom said
and let go
his precious Scots cookies
near to whole
like a molten archipelago
on rainy cobbles.

IV Hootie Bill Do Polonius

T-bone rare
and a side of brain stirfried

is how we liked it
and that's how it'd come out

the both *t*'s crossed, *i*'s dotted
and bloody in between

The weather that year was perfect,
or almost

As for the sun,
you could edge toward the foliage

or no
We were thoroughly rich and young

and the ladies' legs kept on   and on
like Texas

also, they knew tricks

Son,
we were the cutting edge

knew it
and wore it as befits self-knowledge

What got it in the end was filth,
a septic rage

You either flood those critters from the get-go
with the meanest dose

your Daddy makes
or you can kiss that happy nest of good bye-bye

and bye-bye to a most galuptious scene, kid
very

Before Winter

The bugs that swarmed up toward the sun

after the storm
drifting in through the window
and out
into perfumed light

just as the raccoon appears late in August
making the cat wild
who would nest close by him
or bees

coming out in the heat
summerlong after the fog burns off, then return
to the flower pot
half-buried in compost

and now lilac,
impatiens pumping out blooms
even as morning darkens
turns chill

drying their wings in an updraft
ground steaming
after the first big rain knocked off
what of the peaches remained

not knowing what to call them
or the place they rose from

might have let them go by, saying nothing

Before Winter, Part II

Peaches on top of the compost, sitting pretty
rot from underneath blue
— jays swoop
down for poppyseed then curl
back up to the fencepost
because cat
he's got a lot of tricks, funny
angles and spots
he'll come out at you from

if a peach hasn't
brained him yet the way the fool
sleeps chin to dirt
right underneath the damn tree's
big fat peaches too hard
and no good to eat, rotting from the bottom up
nematodes, sowbugs
larvaemites&spores slap-
happy, feasting on sugar

cook the heap of pith, stalk and leaf
so cat 'll sleep warm
between rosemary and the nasturtium
drinking nitrogen
at its base hoping mice or crickets or
some kind of electric
shifts an ion in his whisker
opening one eye as snails both sides
of him, above and below

lay their trails down in the night

Before Winter, Part III

Another six peaches down in the night
and yellowjackets
swarming a rat my darling
boy got hold of
that *pockateeka*, chewing himself
in the shade
o, don't you
sting my good boy's tongue
and leave him choke, no
he is my joy
as day breaks
warm waves of it
first one then the next then the . . . .
each freighted,
denser than the last,
with pieces of night,
of day:
       the aroma of asphalt steaming
after a rain
and the corner vedette
fussing with a pear from the bin, or how
you touched me right then . . .
and faces
voices issuing from those faces
running up&down
the vibraphone of me in dissonant
sheets and there's my

own voice, somehow
got separated in the crowd
I say
    Let me see down from a
very high place,
not tethered here by need

I tell my boy
        Be careful,
manjelaketta,
take especial care
the yard is too too wild

Lint

Ill humours dwell in the upholstery of old men,
but no one comes round anyhow
except Mike from downstairs
who takes a twenty
and only comes back with a fifth of rye.

It's not the window stuck closed
or the dust;
not the gray, crummy shorts —
even in May their b.o. is unemphatic.
It's not the cans of haddie and corn
left half-eaten in the sink;
a sick old belly doesn't want the work.

It's really almost nothing at all
except for the whiskey,
then the naps that fall into naps from afternoon
until daybreak
when the streetlamps begin flickering off
and a full bladder hurts him awake.

Hack

Pigman dispatches us across the city
as barmen shout *last call*.
In a tiny room above Foo Hong's he sweats.

Only the men with eyes of glue are left.
A kid gusts past, smoking
staccato in his fan-tailed old heap.

The Pig tells a joke, something
about one of the dwarves and Snow White,
a vile, Pig sort of joke;

but the vileness recedes, leaving behind
an image of the two of them:
naked, breathless, limbs entwined,

free now of the story's landscape,

dissolving into night.

Song

You see,
it's watts.
                What?
Information, heat
kindling parched stalks — a bush

fire, I mean brush

I mean

like a pretty smile
's
  attached to

              fire . . .

News that stays news.

Art&Life

That's really quite a lovely figure
you bring off
with those several morphemes
arrayed so that when taken up by the mind
they deploy into a kind of umbrella
ranged round an emotion
fleeting and delicate as to seem
the afterimage of an emotion
or of a dream perhaps
or nothing at all,
but always with that high finish,
your signature —
the delightful origami of an exiled prince.

But not nearly so good as
the face
of the Italian beauty, a TV star
on a warm morning
in an alley below Mission, smelling
something much too intimate
underneath the smells of a poor, close street
with its clotheslines, warm brick
and radios pouring
out dj Spanglish, trumpets and love songs

while the dark, blocky girl,
cheekbones and features of an ancient
stone mask, walks past
with her baby, sneaking a look
at those darling lace half-socks, little
tits pushed up high, and hair teased
same as the photos in beauty
parlor windows.
                     — *Another side*
of the city,
        I tell the Signora,
uno altro aspetto.
              Her eyes
gone a bit wild, and the mouth

not so nice.

Since You Didn't Phone

What I had wanted was to be chaste,
sober and uncomfortable
for a sprawling episode on a beach somewhere
dirty, perennially out of fashion;
let the smell of cocoa butter drive deep memory wild
as the sun goes down through a bottle of pop
some kid half-left to turn warm in the sand.

The train ride would be long and hot,
and you've had it with men.
Me . . .
      I'm sickened by the pronoun.
Tenderness seems as far away as Sioux City
and besides, it would have cost too much.
But you should have called,

if only since a preposterous little bout like this
is just the stuff to scare off extra friends,
like soaking their laps with corrosive fizz.
And us . . .
      What an impertinence, *us*.

We could have played gin rummy and taken a stroll
into town or along the boardwalk, maybe
      with dear old Godzilla
rising one last time
over the horizon at dusk, hurrying us to a place
we never would have dreamt of
going.

Sunset in Chinatown

The massive cable turns on its spool, pulling
carloads of tourists to the city's crest

        as the sun sits low
in the hills above Chinatown, exploding

suddenly in the window of Goey Loy Meats, high
along the top of the glass,

showering light over barbecued ducks —

a somehow elegiac splash
this evening, the last week before Labor Day

as if summer, in tandem with the sun,
were being pulled down

and away from us by the great spool's turning.

Thus, the sullen old man in his Mao cap
plucks the zither for change

on a crate outside the geegaw shop:

first, the ancient *Song of Cascading Water,*
followed by the plaintive
        Lament of the Empress Ch'ou

and even the bad little boy from Wichita Falls
trailing behind his parents in a sulk

registers that twinge

birds in the sky, insects and beasts no less
than the Immortals

feel

when the plangent notes take shape in the air,
aligning their souls with Heaven and Earth.